CONTENTS

Readers' Note

**For those readers who have no experience in ecology
and who have not got access to basic laboratory
equipment, there is a special section at the
back of this book.**

This includes notes on:
**1. Simple equipment for making and identifying a collection
2. Using plant and animal identification keys
3. Food chains in a habitat**

ECOLOGY HANDBOOK

O'BRIEN EDUCATIONAL 11 CLARE ST. DUBLIN 2

THE CURRICULUM DEVELOPMENT UNIT

The Curriculum Development Unit was established in September 1972. It is sponsored by the City of Dublin Vocational Education Committee and works in co-operation with the School of Education in Trinity College, Dublin, with the approval of the Department of Education. It has a steering committee composed of representatives of these three bodies. The unit has concentrated on the curricular areas of Science, Humanities and Outdoor Education. The Unit Director is Anton Trant.

I.S.C.I.P. Co-Ordinators

Bryan Powell (1972-1974)

Melvin Freestone (1972-1975)

Bride Rosney (1975 -   )

The materials have been edited for publication by Bride Rosney.

Prior to publication, the following schools were involved in the development, use and revision of the collection. The suggestions and comments of the teachers in these schools have been used as a basis for the edition:

Colaiste Dhulaigh, Coolock; Colaiste Eoin, Finglas; Comprehensive School, Ballymun; Dominican Convent, Ballyfermot; Scoil Ide, Finglas; St. Louise's Secondary School, Ballyfermot; Vocational School, Ballyfermot; Vocational School for Boys, Clogher Road; Colaiste Eanna, Cabra; Coolmine Community School, Clonsilla; Dominican College, Eccles Street; Gonzaga College, Dublin; St. Patrick's Comprehensive School, Shannon; Vocational School, Ringsend; Community School, Tallaght; Newpark Comprehensive School, Blackrock; Vocational School, Killester; Ashton Comprehensive School, Cork; Christian Brothers College, Cork; Mayfield Community School, Cork; Pobal Scoil Iosa, Malahide; Vocational School, Crumlin Road.

ACKNOWLEDGEMENTS

We would like to thank the following for work in the development of the project: Mary Barrett, Kristine Bridges, Mairin Hughes, Brian Kavanagh, Pat Keating, Tom Leonard, Peter MacMenamin, John Markham, David Meehan, Alan Monnelly, Bernard O'Flaherty, Sean O'Riordan, Norman Hickin and Adrian Slattery.

First published 1977. Reprinted 1978.
O'Brien Educational
11 Clare Street, Dublin 2, Ireland.
© *Copyright reserved*

What is Ecology?

The study of how living and non-living things affect or interact with each other is called ecology. So when you study ecology you must study both living and non-living things. Every living thing is found in the surroundings to which it is best suited. For example, we find the earthworm living in soil.

We call the places where plants and animals live together a *habitat*. A habitat can be very large, e.g. the sea, a forest, a desert or even a city. But a habitat may also be quite small, e.g. a fallen tree trunk, the garden rubbish heap or even under one stone.

When studying ecology it is usual to study one particular habitat at a time. To do this you must visit the habitat and make a collection of the different types of plants and animals in the area. It is important to take only one specimen of each organism. Bring the collection back to the laboratory and sort the various species into suitable containers. The keys and diagrams in this book should help you identify each organism.

It is important to keep careful records of your study. Plastic bags and containers used during field work and in the laboratory should be clearly labelled to help you do this. The information you should have includes:

a) Map and geographical details of the area studied.

b) List of all the organisms found and the places where they were found marked in on the map.

c) Diagrams and notes on selected individual species. The notes should detail any special features of the organism which show adaptation to its environment.

d) A diagram of some food chains or food pyramids from the habitat.

e) An idea of the numbers of any particular organism in the habitat. A simple method of recording these numbers is to use a code:

1 = rare, 2 = frequent, 3 = common, 4 = abundant.

From studying one or more habitats in detail you should be able to understand some of the complex relationships between organisms and their environment, and the interdependence of plants and animals.

POINTS TO REMEMBER
when making a collection

1. Always try to keep the habitat in its natural state. When you turn over stones etc., put them back exactly as you found them. Any organisms removed from the habitat should be returned, if possible, after identification and recording.

2. When making your collection, pick up only one specimen of each animal. Never uproot a plant, take one or two leaves only. Don't take any flowers unless they are plentiful.

3. Always keep "sticky" and dry organisms in separate containers.

4. Note the place where each organism is found.

5. Bring back a sample of water and mud or soil from the area in which you make your collection. Microscopic organisms will usually be found in these samples.

EQUIPMENT
for making a collection

To study a habitat properly, it is necessary to identify as many of the organisms as possible. The best way to do this is to make a collection from the habitat. The following pieces of equipment will help you to do this.

1. **A pooter** is used for collecting very small animals. To use the pooter you put the end marked "A" very close to the animal you are trying to capture, and then suck through "B".

The gauze will prevent you from swallowing the organism.

2. **A trowel** is used to dig and sort through soil, sand or mud.

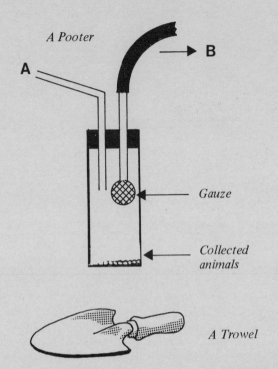

A Pooter

Gauze

Collected animals

A Trowel

3. **A scraper** is used to get living things from places your hand can't reach. For example, under bark and in small cracks of rocks.

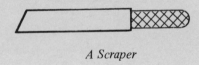

A Scraper

4. **A net** – Two types of nets are useful:

A coarse net is used to sweep through long grass and collect small animals.

A plankton net is used to collect very small animals found in water.

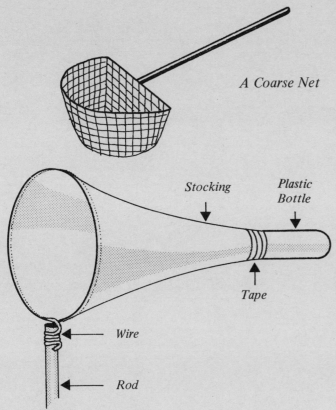

A Coarse Net

Stocking

Plastic Bottle

Tape

Wire

Rod

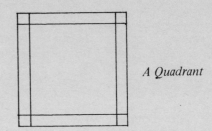

A Quadrant

5. A large white cloth is used to collect small animals that live in trees and shrubs. Spread the sheet under the bush or tree. Shake the tree vigorously.

Collect the animals that fall onto the cloth with a pooter.

6. A quadrant is used to do a quantitative study i.e. to find out how many organisms of one species are present in a particular area. By throwing the quadrant randomly, and counting the number of organisms in the area covered by the quadrant, an ecologist can work out the approximate number in any given area of the habitat.

7. Containers. The living things that ecologists collect are best stored in labelled plastic bags and corked specimen tubes, depending on size.

The labels should be simple enough to fill in when the animal is put into the container, but must contain all the relevant information available.

It is not necessary to put your name and the name of the place you found the organism, if you are studying one habitat only and minding your own collection.

Name:	Limpet
Found:	On sea (east) side of rock. Middle shore.
Quantity:	Large number of them.

8. A sieve. An ordinary kitchen sieve can be used to collect animals from mud or sand. The mud can be collected in the sieve and 'washed' several times with water. The mud will pass through the sieve while the animals remain behind.

EQUIPMENT
for identifying your collection

When you bring your collection back to the laboratory you will need the following equipment to help you sort out, store and identify the organisms.

1. A variety of dishes — plastic basins, white enamel dishes, petri-dishes, glass troughs, beakers etc.

2. Hand lenses, or a binocular microscope of magnification x 10, to help you see the different parts of a small animal more clearly.

3. A microscope, the small objective lens will probably be the most useful, to help you see and identify any microscopic organisms you have collected.

4. Forceps and eye droppers to help you handle the small (including microscopic) organisms.

5. Filter paper strips soaked in alcohol, which are used to "knock-out" small animals.

6. Classification keys.

IDENTIFYING THE ORGANISMS
in your collection

In order to cope with the huge number of organisms known, a biologist sorts out plants and animals into groups (phyla). Similar animals are grouped together and kept separate from totally different ones. This process is called *classification*. So when you identify any organism you are in fact classifying it as belonging to a particular group. Special lists of clues, called keys, will help you identify organisms (see pages 7 and 8). There are also special keys to help you identify animals found in different habitats under each habitat section of this handbook.

When using these special keys you follow the key as usual until you come to a name for a phylum or class.

Underneath the drawing are five pieces of information about the animal:

1. Name of the animal.
2. Type of surroundings the animal is found in.
3. What the animal eats.
4. What the animal is eaten by.
5. The approximate size of the animal.

Note: The drawings are not to scale.

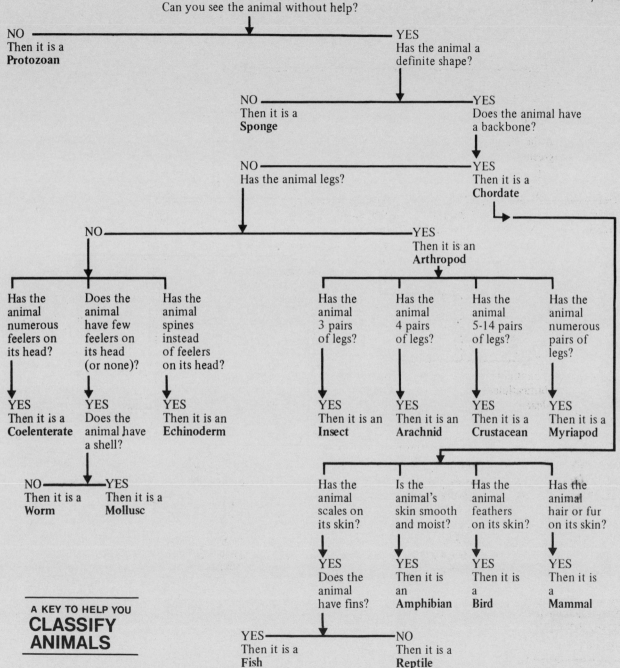

Can you see the animal without help?

NO
Then it is a
Protozoan

YES
Has the animal
a definite shape?

NO
Then it is a
Sponge

YES
Does the animal have
a backbone?

NO
Has the animal legs?

YES
Then it is a
Chordate

NO

YES
Then it is an
Arthropod

Has the
animal
numerous
feelers on
its head?

Does the
animal
have few
feelers on
its head
(or none)?

Has the
animal
spines
instead
of feelers
on its head?

Has the
animal
3 pairs
of legs?

Has the
animal
4 pairs
of legs?

Has the
animal
5-14 pairs
of legs?

Has the
animal
numerous
pairs of
legs?

YES
Then it is a
Coelenterate

YES
Does the
animal have
a shell?

YES
Then it is an
Echinoderm

YES
Then it is an
Insect

YES
Then it is an
Arachnid

YES
Then it is a
Crustacean

YES
Then it is a
Myriapod

NO
Then it is a
Worm

YES
Then it is a
Mollusc

Has the
animal
scales on
its skin?

Is the
animal's
skin smooth
and moist?

Has the
animal
feathers
on its skin?

Has the
animal
hair or fur
on its skin?

YES
Does the
animal
have fins?

YES
Then it is
an
Amphibian

YES
Then it is
a
Bird

YES
Then it is
a
Mammal

A KEY TO HELP YOU
**CLASSIFY
ANIMALS**

YES
Then it is a
Fish

NO
Then it is a
Reptile

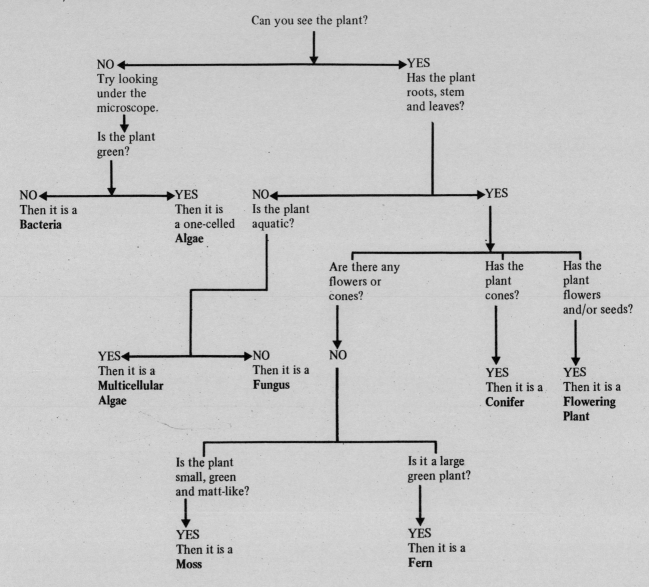

**General Key for
IDENTIFYING
PLANTS**

TERRESTRIAL ECOLOGY

There is a huge variety of terrestrial habitats which can be investigated easily and successfully. School grounds, hedgerows, parks and even garden walls or paths have communities of plants and animals.

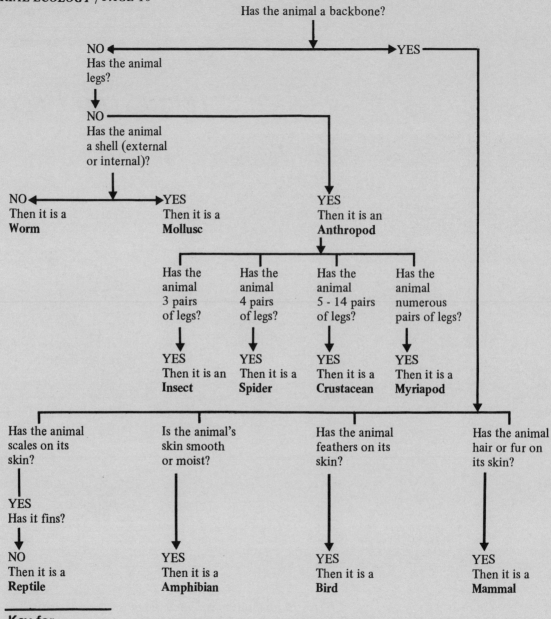

Has the animal a backbone?

NO
Has the animal legs?

YES

NO
Has the animal a shell (external or internal)?

YES
Then it is an
Anthropod

NO
Then it is a
Worm

YES
Then it is a
Mollusc

Has the animal 3 pairs of legs?

Has the animal 4 pairs of legs?

Has the animal 5 - 14 pairs of legs?

Has the animal numerous pairs of legs?

YES
Then it is an
Insect

YES
Then it is a
Spider

YES
Then it is a
Crustacean

YES
Then it is a
Myriapod

Has the animal scales on its skin?

Is the animal's skin smooth or moist?

Has the animal feathers on its skin?

Has the animal hair or fur on its skin?

YES
Has it fins?

NO
Then it is a
Reptile

YES
Then it is a
Amphibian

YES
Then it is a
Bird

YES
Then it is a
Mammal

**Key for
TERRESTRIAL
ANIMALS`**

WORMS

ROUNDWORM
Found in   soil
Eats   is herbiverous, carnivorous, parasitic, or deposit feeder
Eaten by   carnivores
Size   up to 10 mm

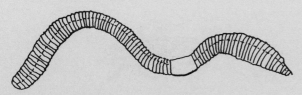

EARTHWORM (rings along body)
Found in   soil
Eats   dead plants
Eaten by   birds
Size   up to 300 mm

INSECTS

Insects – Larval Forms

CATERPILLAR
Found on   plants
Eats   leaves of plants
Eaten by   birds, beetles, ants.
Size   25 - 50 mm

Insects – Adult Forms – with no wings

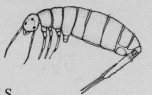

SPRINGTAILS
Found in   soil and leaf litter
Eats   fungi and dead leaves
Eaten by   ground beetles and harvestmen
Size   1 - 2 mm

BRISTLE TAILS
Found on   ground, under bark of trees, in leaf litter
Eats   decaying plant material
Eaten by   small birds
Size   5 - 20 mm

Insects – Adult Forms – with one pair of wings

HOVERFLY
Found on   and hovering around plants
Eats   plant material
Eaten by   birds
Size   up to 10 mm

Insects continued

Insects — Adult Forms — with two pairs of wings top pair hardened

HOUSEFLY
Found in   many places
Eats   organic material
Eaten by   spiders
Size   up to 10 mm

LADYBIRD (Beetle)
Found on   plants
Eats   aphids (greenfly)
Eaten by   birds
Size   5 - 10 mm

ROBBER FLY
Found in   grass and trees
Eats   other insects
Eaten by   spiders
Size   20 - 30 mm

SOLDIER BEETLE
Found on   plants
Eats   other insects
Eaten by   birds
Size   5 - 10 mm

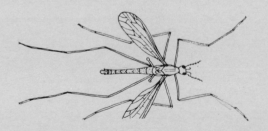

GNAT-LIKE FLY — CRANE FLY (Daddy Longlegs)
Found in   grass
Eats   organic material
Eaten by   spiders
Size   40 mm

WEEVIL
Found on   trees, bushes
Eats   fruits and seeds
Eaten by   birds
Size   10 mm

GROUND BEETLE
Found   under logs, stones
Eats   small animals e.g. insect larvae
Eaten by birds
Size   10 - 15 mm

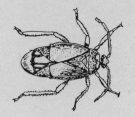

CAPSID BUG
Found in trees and bushes
Eats   fruit and seeds
Eaten by beetles and small birds
Size   15 mm

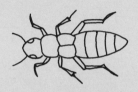

DEVIL'S COACH HORSE BEETLE
Found in rotting plants, under stones
           dead animals, near animal dung,
Eats   insect larvae and small insects
Eaten by birds
Size   25 mm

SHIELD BUG
Found in trees, bushes and herbs
Eats   fruit, leaves and sucks plant sap
Eaten by small birds
Size   15 - 20 mm

———

*Insects — Adult Forms — with two pairs of wings —
top pair not completely hardened*

*Insects — Adult Forms — with two pairs of wings —
wings large and scaly*

GREEN APHID (Greenfly)
Found in trees, bushes and herbs
Eats   is a sapsucker
Eaten by beetles, ladybirds
Size   5 mm

MOTH
Found in bushes, trees
Eats   nectar of flowers
Eaten by small birds
Size   5 - 60 mm

Insects continued

BUTTERFLY
Found in	flowers, bushes and grass
Eats	nectar of flowers
Eaten by	small birds
Size	20 - 70 mm *(wingspan measurement)*

HONEYBEE
Found in	flowers and bushes
Eats	nectar of flowers
Eaten by	small birds
Size	15 mm

Insects – Adult Forms – with two pairs of wings – both pairs membranous

ANT
Found in	ground, trees and grass
Eats	scavenger and also eats insect larvae and bugs
Eaten by	beetles and small birds
Size	5 - 10 mm

WASP
Found in	flowers and bushes
Eats	plant material
Eaten by	birds
Size	20 mm

LACEWING
Found in	bushes and trees
Eats	predator on aphids and leaf hoppers
Eaten by	spiders and small birds
Size	10 - 15 mm

BUMBLE BEE
Found in	flowers and bushes
Eats	nectar of flowers
Eaten by	small birds
Size	25 mm

OTHER INSECTS

GRASSHOPPER
Found in   grass and small plants
Eats   mainly grass
Eaten by   small birds
Size   25 mm

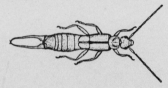

EARWIG
Found in   ground, bushes
Eats   carnivorous – eats dead animals
Eaten by   small birds
Size   15 - 20 mm

SPIDERS

MITE
Found on   ground and in leaf litter
Eats   leaf litter
Eaten by   small birds, harvestmen and beetles
Size   Up to 5 mm

SPIDER
Found on   trees and grass
Eats   insects
Eaten by   small birds
Size   7 mm

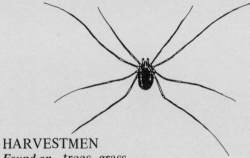

HARVESTMEN
Found on   trees, grass
Eats   insects and mites
Eaten by   small birds
Size   7 mm

CRUSTACEA

WOOD LOUSE
Found in   logs, under stones, bark of old trees
Eats   rotting wood and leaf litter
Eaten by   beetles and small birds
Size   10 mm

MYRIAPODA

SNAKE MILLIPEDE
Found in   ground under trees
Eats   decaying plants
Eaten by   small birds
Size   30 mm

PILL MILLIPEDE
Found in   ground under trees
Eats   decaying leaves
Eaten by   small birds
Size   10 mm

MOLLUSCA

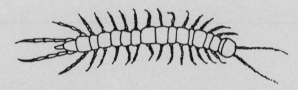

CENTIPEDE
Found in   dead trees and under stones
Eats   carnivorous — eats insects and spiders
Eaten by   small birds
Size   20 mm

COMMON GARDEN SNAIL
Found in   grass, ground, bushes *(usually wet areas)*
Eats   leaves
Eaten by   birds
Size   60 mm

FLAT-BACK MILLIPEDE
Found in   under stones, under bark
Eats   decaying plants
Eaten by   small birds
Size   25 mm

GREY FIELD SLUG
Found in   ground, grass, bushes
Eats   plants
Eaten by   birds and frogs
Size   60 mm

AMPHIBIA

FROG
Found in wet places
Eats small insects, spiders, slugs and worms
Eaten by ducks and other birds
Size 150 mm (approx.)

MAMMALS

FIELD MOUSE
Found in shrubs, grasses
Eats fruit, seeds, fungi, insects and snails
Eaten by large carnivores e.g. owls, crows, foxes, stoats
Size 80 mm (body length)

AVES (birds)

Swallow

Cuckoo

AVES (birds)

Robin

Sparrow

Magpie

Thrush

PLANTS

Fungi:
Mushroom

Ferns:

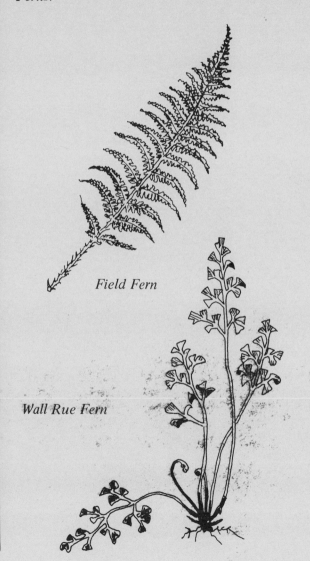

Field Fern

Mosses:

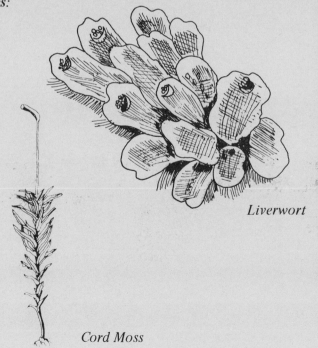

Liverwort

Wall Rue Fern

Cord Moss

Conifers

Larch

Spruce

Scots Pine

Cypress

Yew

PLANTS

Flowering Plants: Woody

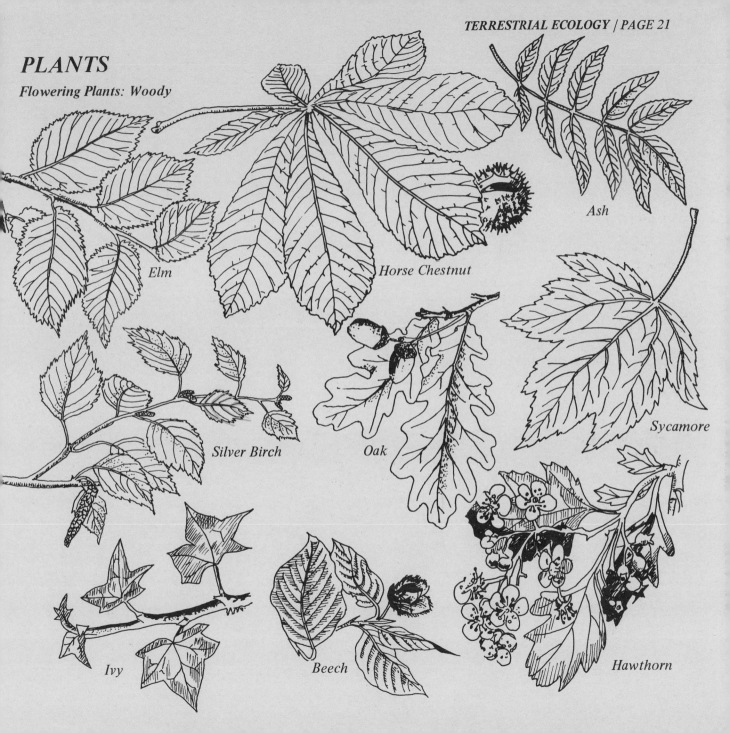

Elm

Horse Chestnut

Ash

Silver Birch

Oak

Sycamore

Ivy

Beech

Hawthorn

Flowering Plants: Not woody

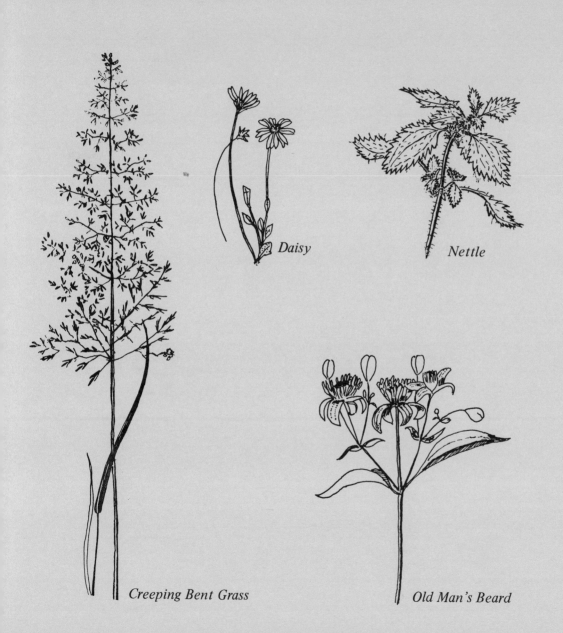

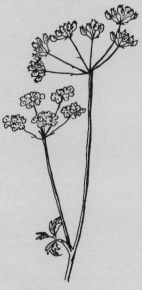

Daisy

Nettle

Dandelion

Creeping Bent Grass

Old Man's Beard

Hedge Parsley

Grounsel

Coltsfoot

Thistle

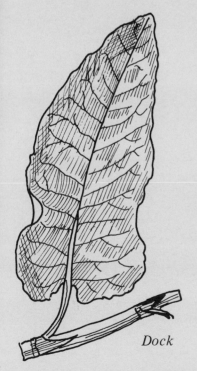

Dock

Ragwort

Elder

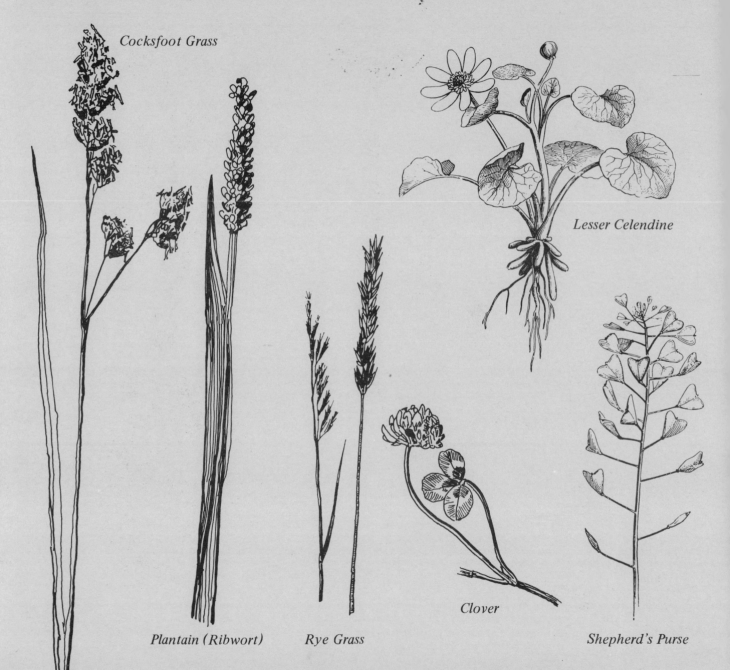

Cocksfoot Grass

Lesser Celendine

Plantain (Ribwort)

Rye Grass

Clover

Shepherd's Purse

SEASHORE ECOLOGY

The rocky seashore is one of the most suitable habitats for school ecology studies. There is a large variety of organisms present and the shore can be divided into areas or zones:

High tide zone : Covered by spring tides only
Mid tide zone : Covered and uncovered every day
Low tide zone : Uncovered by spring tides only

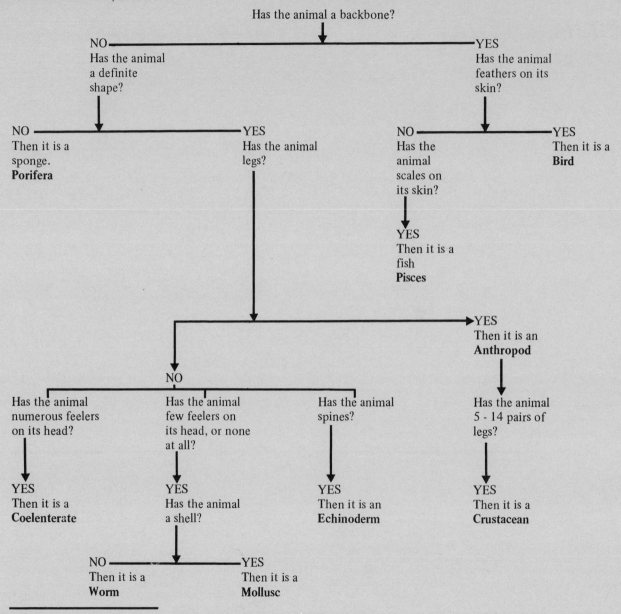

Has the animal a backbone?

NO — Has the animal a definite shape?

YES — Has the animal feathers on its skin?

NO — Then it is a sponge. **Porifera**

YES — Has the animal legs?

NO — Has the animal scales on its skin?

YES — Then it is a **Bird**

YES — Then it is a fish **Pisces**

YES — Then it is an **Anthropod**

NO

Has the animal numerous feelers on its head?

Has the animal few feelers on its head, or none at all?

Has the animal spines?

Has the animal 5 - 14 pairs of legs?

YES — Then it is a **Coelenterate**

YES — Has the animal a shell?

YES — Then it is an **Echinoderm**

YES — Then it is a **Crustacean**

NO — Then it is a **Worm**

YES — Then it is a **Mollusc**

Key for SEASHORE ANIMALS

PORIFERA
(sponges)

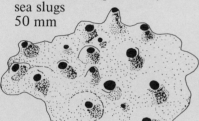

PURSE SPONGE (white/yellow)
Found on   lower shore
Eats   filter feeder   (plankton)
Eaten by sea slugs
Size   50 mm

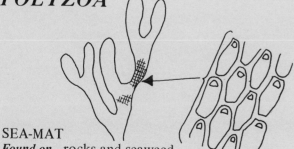

BREADCRUMB SPONGE (green/yellow)
Found on   lower shore
Eats   filter feeder (plankton)
Eaten by sea slugs
Size   75 mm

POLYZOA

SEA-MAT
Found on   rocks and seaweed
Eats   filter feeder (plankton)
Eaten by winkles, top shells and limpets
Size   structure is microscopic

COELENTERATES

HYDROID
Found on   lower shore
Eats   filter feeder (small planktonic crustacea)
Eaten by sea slugs
Size   3 - 5 mm

SEA ANEMONE
Found on   lower shore in rock pools
Eats   shrimps, prawns, fish
Eaten by carnivores e.g. sea slugs
Size   5 - 20 mm

JELLYFISH
Found on   water's edge
Eats   plankton and even small fish depending on size
Eaten by carnivores
Size   75 - 300 mm

WORMS

SPIROBIS
Found in   hard tubes on sea weed and rocks
Eats   filter feeder (plankton)
Eaten by   carnivores
Size   ½ - 1 mm

RAGWORM
Found on   seashore (sand)
Eats   animals in sand and dead material
Eaten by   birds
Size   125 mm

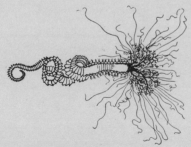

SANDMASON (bristle worm)
Found on   seashore (sand)
Eats   filter feeder (plankton)
Eaten by   other worms, dogwhelks and birds
Size   150 - 175 mm

CRUSTACEA

COMMON SHORE CRAB
Found on   any part of the shore, in rock pools,
           under stones, on sea-weed
Eats   scavenger - remains of dead animals
Eaten by   birds, fish, other crabs when moulting
Size   100 mm

PORCELAIN CRAB
Found on   lower shore
Eats   scavenger - remains of dead animals
Eaten by   birds, fish, other crabs when moulting
Size   25 mm

HERMIT CRAB
Found in   Middle and lower shore, in rock pools
          and under stones
Eats   scavenger, and filter feeder
Eaten by   birds, fish and other crabs when moulting
Size   up to 25 mm

Crustacea continued

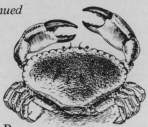

EDIBLE CRAB
Found on middle and lower shore, among seaweed
Eats scavenger
Eaten by birds, fish, and other crabs when moulting
Size up to 250 mm

PRAWN
Found in rock pools
Eats algae and small crustacea, also scavenges
Eaten by carnivores - e.g. anemones
Size up to 100 mm

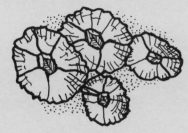

BARNACLE
Found on middle and lower shore
Eats filter feeder (plankton)
Eaten by dog whelks and birds
Size 10 - 15 mm

MOLLUSCA

ROUGH PERIWINKLE
Found on upper and middle shore, in exposed areas
  on rocks
Eats small algae
Eaten by blenny and dog whelk
Size 5 - 15 mm

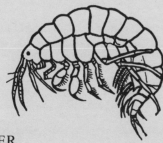

SANDHOPPER
Found on upper shore
Eats mainly algae
Eaten by carnivores e.g. crabs and birds
Size up to 20 mm

FLAT PERIWINKLE
Found on middle and lower shore, in sheltered areas
  on rock and among algae
Eats small algae
Eaten by birds, blenny and dog whelks
Size 15 - 20 mm

Mollusca continued

TOP SHELL
Found on   middle and lower shore on rocks
Eats   small algae
Eaten by   birds
Size   10 - 25 mm

EDIBLE PERIWINKLE
Found on   lower shore on rocks and among algae
Eats   small algae
Eaten by   birds
Size   10 - 25 mm

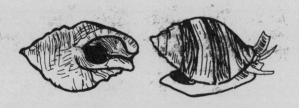

DOG WHELK
Found on   middle and lower shore on rocks
Eats   barnacles, mussels, periwinkles, top shells
Eaten by   birds and fish
Size   25 mm

LIMPET
Found on   middle and lower shore on rocks and in
             exposed areas
Eats   small algae
Eaten by   birds and blenny when dead
Size   15 - 60 mm

MUSSEL
Found on   low and middle shore on rocks and in
             cracks of rocks
Eats   filter feeder
Eaten by   dog whelks and starfish
Size   up to 100 mm

ECHINODERMATA

SEA URCHIN
Found on   lower shore
Eats   algae
Eaten by   carnivores - e.g. starfish
Size   up to 150 mm

Echinodermata continued

BRITTLE STAR
Found on   lower shore
Eats   some are herbivores (eat algae), others are carnivores (eat mussels etc.)
Eaten by   crabs
Size   10 - 25 mm (disc measurement)

STARFISH
Found on   lower shore
Eats   mussels, other bivalves
Eaten by   crabs
Size   100 mm up

PISCES *(fish)*

BLENNY
Found in   pools under stones
Eats   barnacles, periwinkles, limpets etc.
Eaten by   birds
Size   25 - 125 mm

EEL
Found in   rock pools
Eats   plankton or smaller fish
Eaten by   birds
Size   often 2 - 3 metres in length (2000 - 3000 mm)

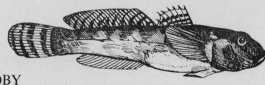

BUTTERFISH
Found on   lower shore in pools under stones
Eats   barnacles, mussels
Eaten by   birds
Size   75 - 200 mm

GOBY
Found in   rock pools
Eats   plankton
Eaten by   birds
Size   150 - 200 mm

AVES (birds)

Seagull

Turn Stone

Great Black Backed Gull

Oyster Catcher

Black Headed Gull

Herring Gull

Cormorant

PLANTS
Brown Algae

Serrated Wrack
Found on: lower shore

Channel Weed
Found on: upper shore

Flat Wrack
Found on: upper shore

Bladder Wrack
Found on: middle shore

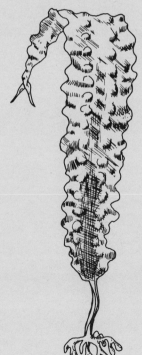

Oarweed
Found on: lower shore

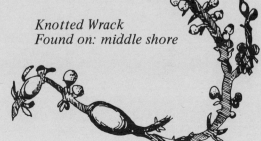

Knotted Wrack
Found on: middle shore

Green Algae

Red Algae

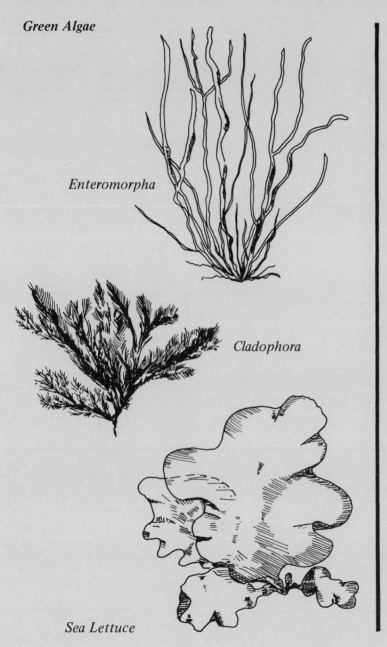

Enteromorpha

Cladophora

Sea Lettuce

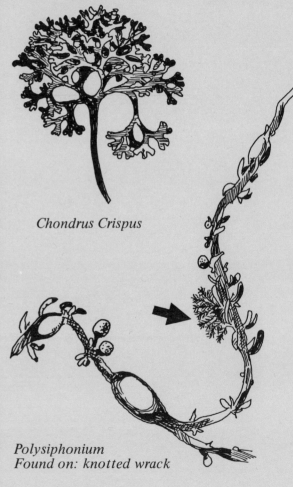

Chondrus Crispus

Polysiphonium
Found on: knotted wrack

FRESHWATER ECOLOGY

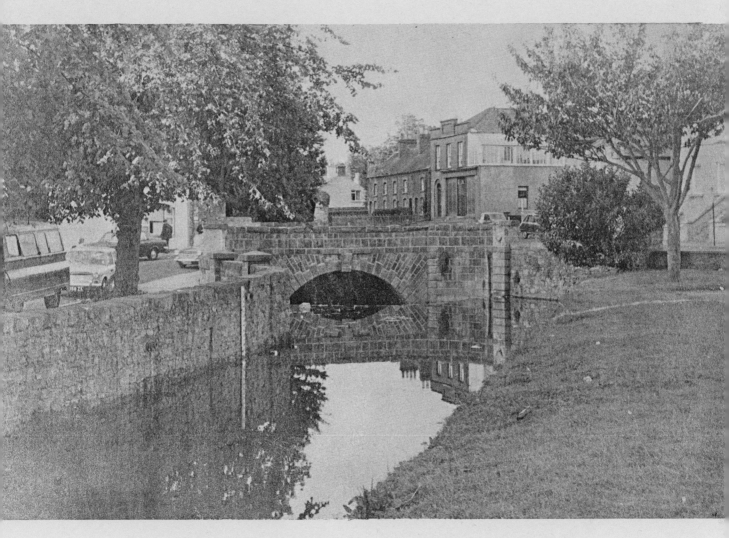

There is usually a freshwater habitat near every school — it may be part of a canal, a lake or a pool. There is generally a wide variety of organisms present in freshwater, but pollution may cause a decrease in numbers and types of organisms.

Has the animal a backbone?

NO
Can the animal be seen clearly without any help?

YES
Is the animal's skin smooth or moist?

NO
Is it divided into many cells?

YES
Has the animal legs?

NO
Has the animal scales on its skin?

YES
Then it is an **Amphibian**

NO
Then it is a **Protozoa**

YES
Then it is a **Coelenterata**

YES
Then it is a **Pisces (fish)**

NO
Has the animal a shell?

YES
Then it is an **Arthropod**

NO
Then it is a **Worm**

YES
Then it is a **Mollusc**

Has the animal 3 pairs of legs?

Has the animal 4 pairs of legs?

Has the animal 5 - 14 pairs of legs?

A key for FRESHWATER ANIMALS

YES
Then it is an **Insect**

YES
Then it is a **Spider**

YES
Then it is a **Crustacea**

PROTOZOA

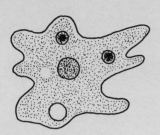

AMOEBA
Found in still freshwater
Eats plankton and other protozoa
Eaten by filter feeders
Size microscopic

PARAMECIUM
Found in stagnant freshwater
Eats plankton
Eaten by filter feeders
Size microscopic

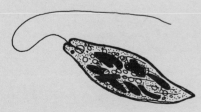

EUGLENA
Found in stagnant freshwater
Eats feeds like a plant - makes its own food
Eaten by filter feeders
Size microscopic

COELENTERATES

HYDRA
Found on water plants in fresh water
Eats small planktonic crustacea
Eaten by insects and crustacean larvae, flatworms
Size 2 - 12 mm

WORMS

FLATWORMS (planaria type)
Found on bottom of ponds and streams
Eats small animals and fish eggs
Eaten by insect larvae, newts and fish
Size 5 - 25 mm

ROUNDWORM
Found on freshwater, sea-shore, soil
Eats is herbivorous, carnivorous, parasitic, or
        deposit feeder
Eaten by carnivores
Size 1 - 10 mm

Worms continued

MIDGE LARVA
Found in   still and stagnant water
Eats   decaying plant material
Eaten by   water crickets
Size   6 mm

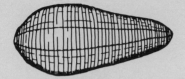

LEECH
Found on   and under stones, among plants or in mud
Eats   body fluids of other animals
Eaten by   carnivores - beetles
Size   10 - 150 mm

———

Insects — Larval Forms

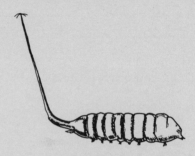

HOVERFLY LARVA (Rat-tailed maggot)
Found in   puddles of stagnant water
Eats   decaying matter
Eaten by   carnivores, larvae and birds
Size   25 - 50 mm

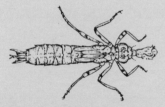

DRAGON FLY LARVA
Found in   still or slow-moving water
Eats   worm and insect larvae
Eaten by   other carnivores - e.g. fish
Size   30 mm

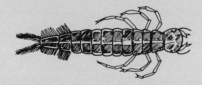

BEETLE LARVA
Found in   still or slow-moving water
Eats   almost any small animal e.g. small fish, worms, tadpoles
Eaten by   other carnivores e.g. fish
Size   up to 40 mm

CADDISFLY LARVA
Found on   bottom of slow-moving or still water
Eats   plant and animal material
Eaten by ·   carnivores e.g. fish, water birds
Size   25 mm

Insects continued

Insects — Adult Forms

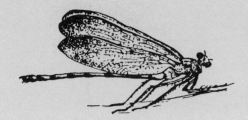

DAMSEL FLY LARVA
Found in   still or slow-moving water
Eats   worms and insect larvae
Eaten by   other carnivores e.g. fish
Size   30 mm

WHIRLIGIG BEETLE
Found on   surface of still and slow-moving water
Eats   insects which fall into the water
Eaten by   fish and birds
Size   7 mm

MAYFLY LARVA
Found in   slow or still-moving water
Eats   algae and plant debris
Eaten by   carnivores e.g. beetle larvae, beetles, fish
Size   20 mm

WATER CRICKET (bug)
Found on   surface of ponds and slow moving streams
Eats   small insects and midges
Eaten by   fish and frogs
Size   8 mm

STONE-FLY LARVA
Found in   running water, streams with gravel bottom
Eats   algae and plant debris
Eaten by   carnivores e.g. beetle larvae, beetles, fish
Size   15 mm

WATER MEASURER (bug)
Found on   surface of still and slow moving water
Eats   water fleas, mosquito larvae and small insects
Eaten by   frogs and fish
Size   10 mm

Insects continued

GREAT SILVER BEETLE
Found in   shallow weedy ponds
Eats   decaying pond plants
Eaten by   fish, frogs and birds
Size   45 mm

POND SLATER (bug)
Found on   surface of still water
Eats   small insects that fall into water
Eaten by   fish and frogs
Size   8 mm

WATER BOATMAN (bug)
Found in   fresh water ponds
Eats   algae and plant debris
Eaten by   frogs
Size   12 mm

SPIDERS

WATER MITE
Found   swimming in fresh water
Eats   small crustacea and other small animals
Eaten by   insect larvae and fish
Size   3 mm

CRUSTACEA

WATER FLEA (planktonic crustacean)
Found in   freshwater
Eats   filter feeder (plankton)
Eaten by   hydra, water mites, fish
Size   microscopic

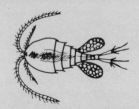

COPEPOD (planktonic crustacean)
Found in   freshwater
Eats   filter feeder
Eaten by   hydra, water mites, fish
Size   microscopic

Crustacea continued

WATER LOUSE
Found in	crawling among plants in freshwater
Eats	dead and decaying plant material
Eaten by	carnivores
Size	12 mm

PEA OR ORB SHELL
Found in	mud in streams
Eats	filter feeder (plankton)
Eaten by	fish
Size	15 mm

MOLLUSCA

AMPHIBIANS

RAMSHORN SNAIL
Found in	still and slow moving water, among thick plant growth
Eats	algae and pond plants
Eaten by	birds and fish
Size	30 mm

FROG
Found	near water, damp places
Eats	small insects, worms and slugs
Eaten by	ducks and other birds
Size	150 mm approx.

POND SNAIL
Found in	large ponds and slow streams
Eats	algae and pond plants
Eaten by	birds and fish
Size	40 mm

NEWT
Found in	plants in still fresh water
Eats	flat worms, small insects, crustaceans, tadpoles
Eaten by	birds
Size	up to 100 mm

PISCES (fish)

STICKLEBACK

Found in	fresh water - except streams and stagnant water
Eats	any small invertebrates e.g. worms, snails, insects
Eaten by	birds
Size	80 - 100 mm

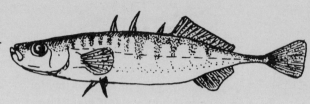

SUBMERGED PLANTS

Canadian Pondweed (Elodea)

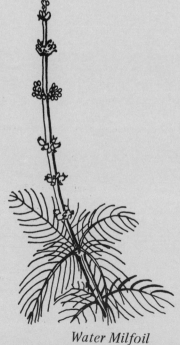

Water Milfoil

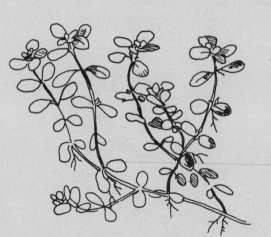

Water Starwort

FLOATING PLANTS

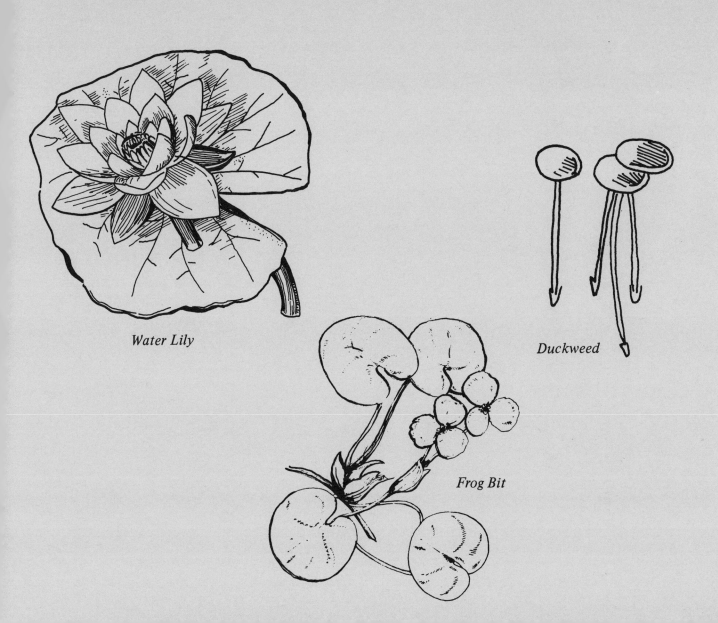

Water Lily

Duckweed

Frog Bit

WATERSIDE PLANTS

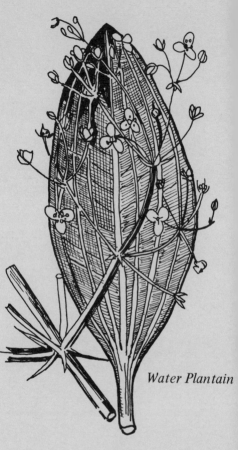

Rushes

Marsh Marigold

Water Plantain

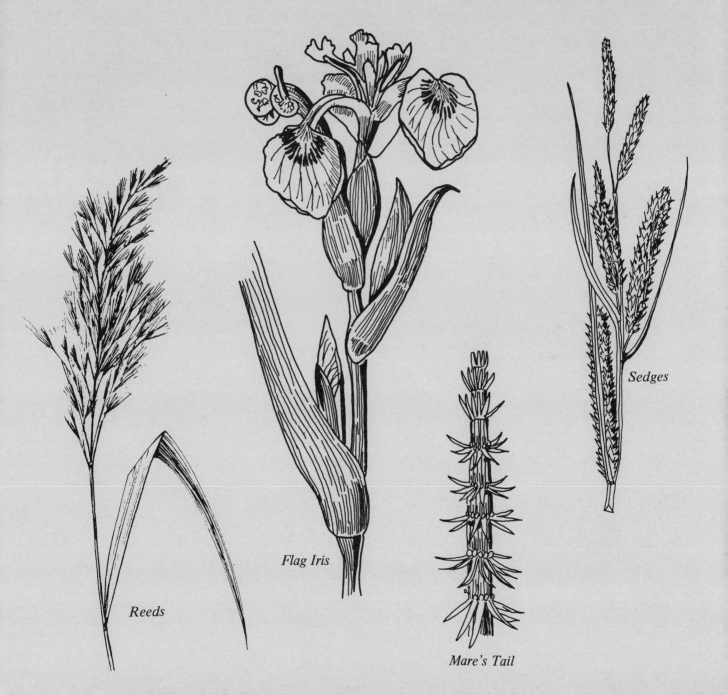

Reeds

Flag Iris

Mare's Tail

Sedges

REFERENCES

Blandford Colour Series: Blandford Press Ltd.

Biology An Environmental Approach, by E. Perrot, E. Martin, J. Watson, D. Hughes-Evans, I. Cambell, and J. Keri-Davies. John Murray, London 1968.

Collins Pocket Guide to the Sea Shore, by J. Barrett and C. M. Young: Collins, Glasgow.

Hulton's Biological Field Studies: Series, by P. M. Miles and H. B. Miles: Hulton Publications Ltd.

Intermediate Biology by B. L. Powell: Allen Figgis, Dublin.

Nuffield Secondary Science - Theme 1: Longman, London.

Practical Biology by B. L. Powell and F. White: Allen Figgis, Dublin.

The Observer's Series: Frederich Warne.

Schools Council, Project Environment: Longman, London.

Study of Life, by D. Goodhue, B. Healy, E. Collen, and E. Okely: Folens, Dublin.

Ladybird Series, Ladybird, London.

Folens Environmental Series, Folens, Dublin.

You will also find interesting sections on ecology in encyclopaedias.

IMPORTANT TERMS AND IDEAS

Adaptation to Environment: This is the special way in which a plant or animal is made so that it can live in its environment. Every living thing is in some way adapted (changed) to suit life in its natural surroundings.

Carnivore: A carnivore is an animal which eats other animals - usually herbivores (plant eaters). They are often called *second order consumers*.

Classification: This is the process by which plants and animals are sorted out into groups. Organisms which have similar characteristics are grouped together.

Class: A phylum is divided up into classes. For example animals belonging to the phylum Artropoda are divided into class insects, class spiders, class crustacea and class myriapoda.

Conservation: Conservation is the way man tries to preserve and maintain the natural conditions of a habitat.

Community: In a habitat plants and animals live together. The plants and animals affect each other in different ways, some depend upon each other for survival, while others compete with each other. The group of plants and animals living in any one place makes up a community of living things.

Environment: The surroundings of an organism are its environment. The environment includes both living and non-living things which have an effect on the development and life of the organism.

Evolution: Evolution is the process by which the huge number of plants and animals in the world today have developed from very simple living things which are thought to have existed about 1000 million years ago. Of the animals you may find, the Protozoa are the simplest and you are the most highly developed.

Food-chains: All living things need food to live. Plants make their own food, animals get their food by eating plants or other animals. Therefore, an animal which eats plants may itself be eaten by other animals. In this way a food chain is built up. Each living thing has its own place or *niche* in a food chain, in which it depends on other things for survival.

Habitat: A habitat is a natural living place of plants and animals.

Herbivore: A herbivore is an animal which eats plants. Plants are often called *primary producers* and the animals that feed on them are called *first order consumers*.

Life-cycle: The different stages in the life of a plant or animal from birth, to growth, to maturity, to reproduction and finally to death is called a life-cycle. Every living thing has its own type of life-cycle. For example, a butterfly grows from an egg into a caterpillar, and then into a crysalis or pupa, and finally into an adult. The adult lays eggs and in this way the cycle is started again.

Natural selection: is the way in which the living things which are best adapted to their surroundings will be the most successful in the competition for survival. Plants and animals which compete best for survival are usually found in the greatest numbers. Natural selection is a controlling factor in evolution.

Parasite: an animal or plant which lives on or in another living thing getting food from its body. A parasite often causes the death of the host organism.

Pollution: When the environment is spoiled or dirtied we say it is polluted. Man is dumping poisonous waste materials into the environment all the time. The poisonous waste kills living things in the habitat. There are many different types of pollution: chemical waste from factories, litter dumped in fields, sewage etc.

Phylum: Animals are grouped, according to their similarities, into 11 phyla. The groupings of plants are called either phyla or divisions.

Scavengers: These are animals that feed on dead material, and sometimes on living things.

Notes for Beginners
and those who have not got access to a laboratory

Simple Equipment

On pages 4-6 there is a description of the equipment necessary to make, and identify, a collection of organisms. This equipment is usually available in a laboratory, but simple alternatives can be found or made at home. *See illustrations on pages 4 and 5.*

A Pooter You can make a pooter using a clear plastic tablet container, a cork and some rubber or plastic tubing. Plastic straws will do if the pooter is only to be used for very tiny animals.

Use a small drill to make holes in the cork — or a cork-screw and small screwdriver. *(See diagram on page 4.)*

A Trowel A garden trowel or small shovel can be used.

A Scraper An old kitchen knife is suitable.

Nets Two types of nets are used:
i) A coarse net — the type you buy at the seaside.
ii) A plankton net — can be made from one leg of an old pair of ladies nylon tights. Cut away the toe and tie on a small plastic tablet container. Sew the other end to a wire hoop fixed to a stick *as in the diagram on page 5.*

Large White Cloth A piece of an old sheet will do.

A Quadrant A quadrant can be made by nailing together (or better still, gluing and screwing) four equal lengths of wood, like rulers, in the form of a square.

Containers Jam jars, tablet containers, plastic basins, etc. are all useful for sorting out a collection.

Magnifying Glass A magnifying glass (hand lens) will help you see many of the parts of an organism clearly. If you can borrow a microscope you should be able to find microscopic organisms in water, mud, etc.

Eyebrow Tweezers A tweezers is helpful when handling small animals.

Alcohol To "knock-out" small animals use cotton wool soaked in alcohol in a tablet container. *(You can get alcohol from a chemist).*

Using plant and animal identification keys

In order to make sense of the great number of plants and animals in the world, a biologist acts like a stamp collector. He sorts out his collection so that similar plants are grouped together and kept quite separate from totally different ones. Animals are also sorted into groups. This process of sorting is called *CLASSIFICATION.*

To help classify plants or animals a biologist uses lists of clues called *KEYS.* The keys on pages 7 and 8 will help you classify any animal or plant into the phylum (group) to which it belongs.

Food chains

Plants can make their own food using sunlight, water and a gas called carbon dioxide which is in air. All animals are directly or indirectly dependant on plants for their food. A food chain gives us information on animals and plants in a habitat by showing us what eats what and what is eaten by what.

The diagrams below illustrate food inter-relationships between plants and animals. You should notice that plants will always be at the bottom of the food chain (or pyramid).

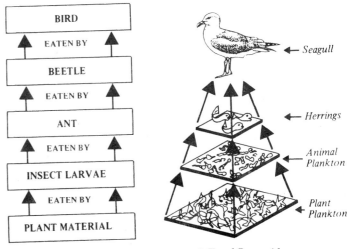

A Food Chain   A Food Pyramid